JESUS
His Life & His Love

Trilogy Christian Publishers
A Wholly Owned Subsidiary of Trinity Broadcasting Network
2442 Michelle Drive
Tustin, CA 92780

Copyright © 2020 by Althea Duren

All Scripture quotations, unless otherwise noted, taken from THE HOLY BIBLE, NEW INTERNATIONAL VERSION®, NIV® Copyright © 1973, 1978, 1984, 2011 by Biblica, Inc.® Used by permission. All rights reserved worldwide.

Scripture quotations marked (KJV) taken from *The Holy Bible, King James Version*. Cambridge Edition: 1769.

All rights reserved, including the right to reproduce this book or portions thereof in any form whatsoever.

For information, address Trilogy Christian Publishing
Rights Department, 2442 Michelle Drive, Tustin, Ca 92780.
Trilogy Christian Publishing/ TBN and colophon are trademarks of Trinity Broadcasting Network.

For information about special discounts for bulk purchases, please contact Trilogy Christian Publishing.

Manufactured in the United States of America

Trilogy Disclaimer: The views and content expressed in this book are those of the author and may not necessarily reflect the views and doctrine of Trilogy Christian Publishing or the Trinity Broadcasting Network.

10 9 8 7 6 5 4 3 2 1

Library of Congress Cataloging-in-Publication Data is available.

ISBN 978-1-64773-432-9 (Print Book)
ISBN 978-1-64773-433-6 (ebook)

JESUS
His Life & His Love

An ABC Rhyme Book

ALTHEA DUREN

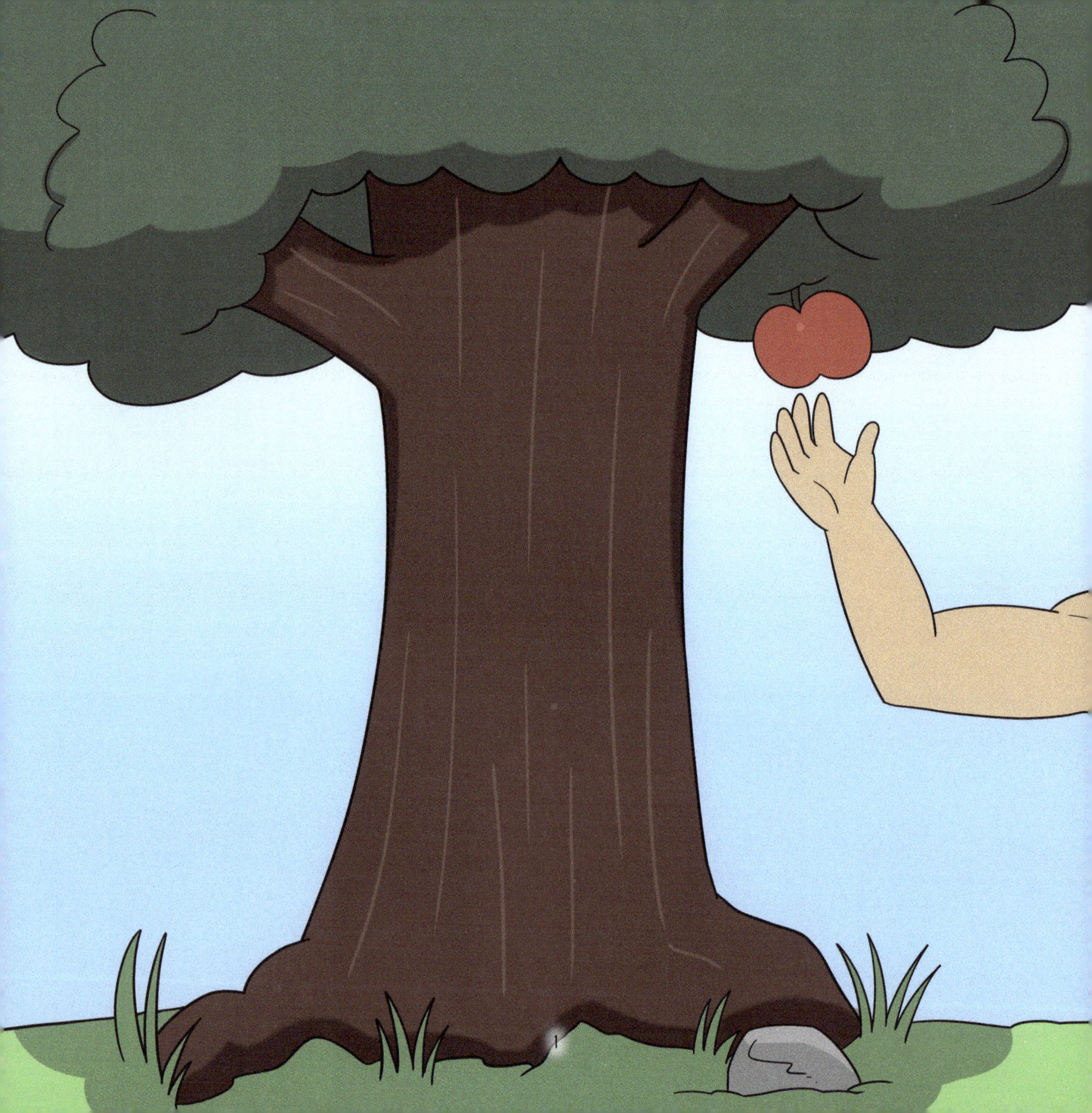

Adam

(Genesis 3:7; John 3:19-21; Acts 26:18; Romans 5:12, 19)

Sin was brought to the world by him,
by taking the fruit off of its stem,
and eating it to his heart's delight,
turned us from God's light to Satan's dark night.

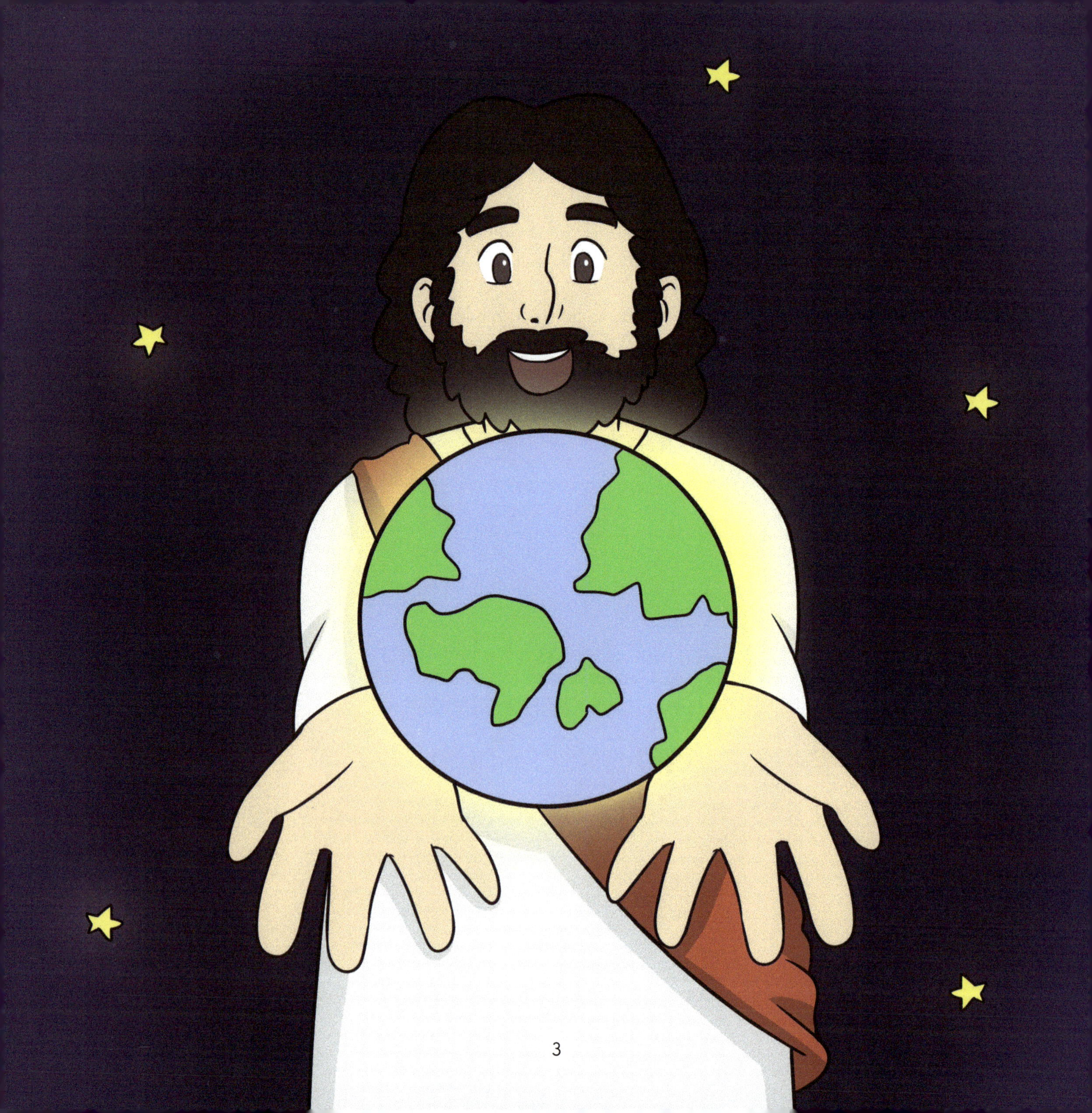

Begotten Son

(John 3:3; John 3:16; I John 4:2)

But God loved us so, that He sent us His Son,
So no one would perish, no not even one.
He was God in the flesh, while He lived on this earth,
His mission to give us all second birth.

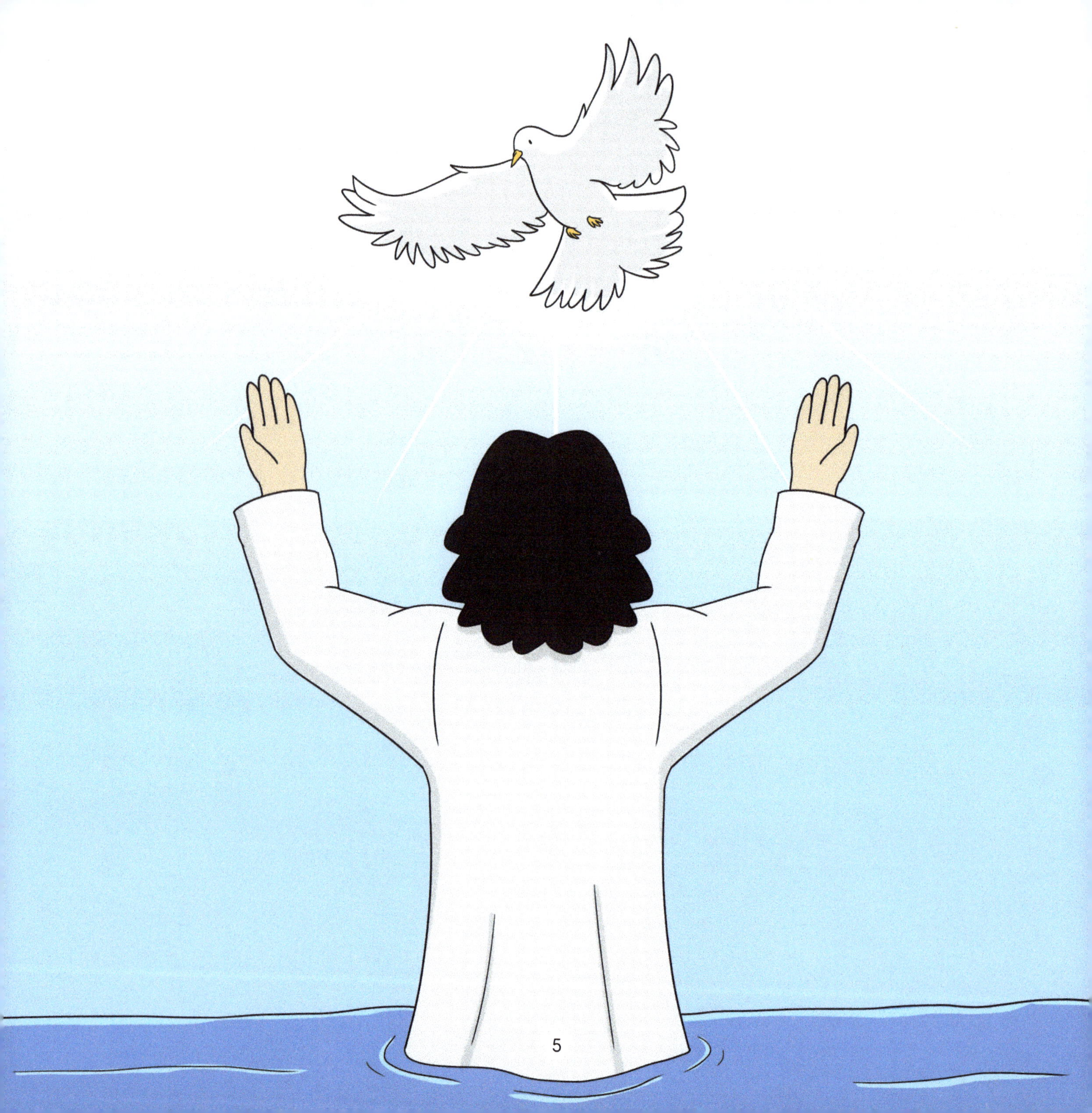

Christ, the Anointed One

(Isaiah 11:1-3; Isaiah 61:1; Luke 4:18, 19)

The fear of the Lord would be His delight.
The Spirit rest on Him with wisdom and might.
He'd spread the good news to the rich and the poor,
and those bound by sin would be free evermore.

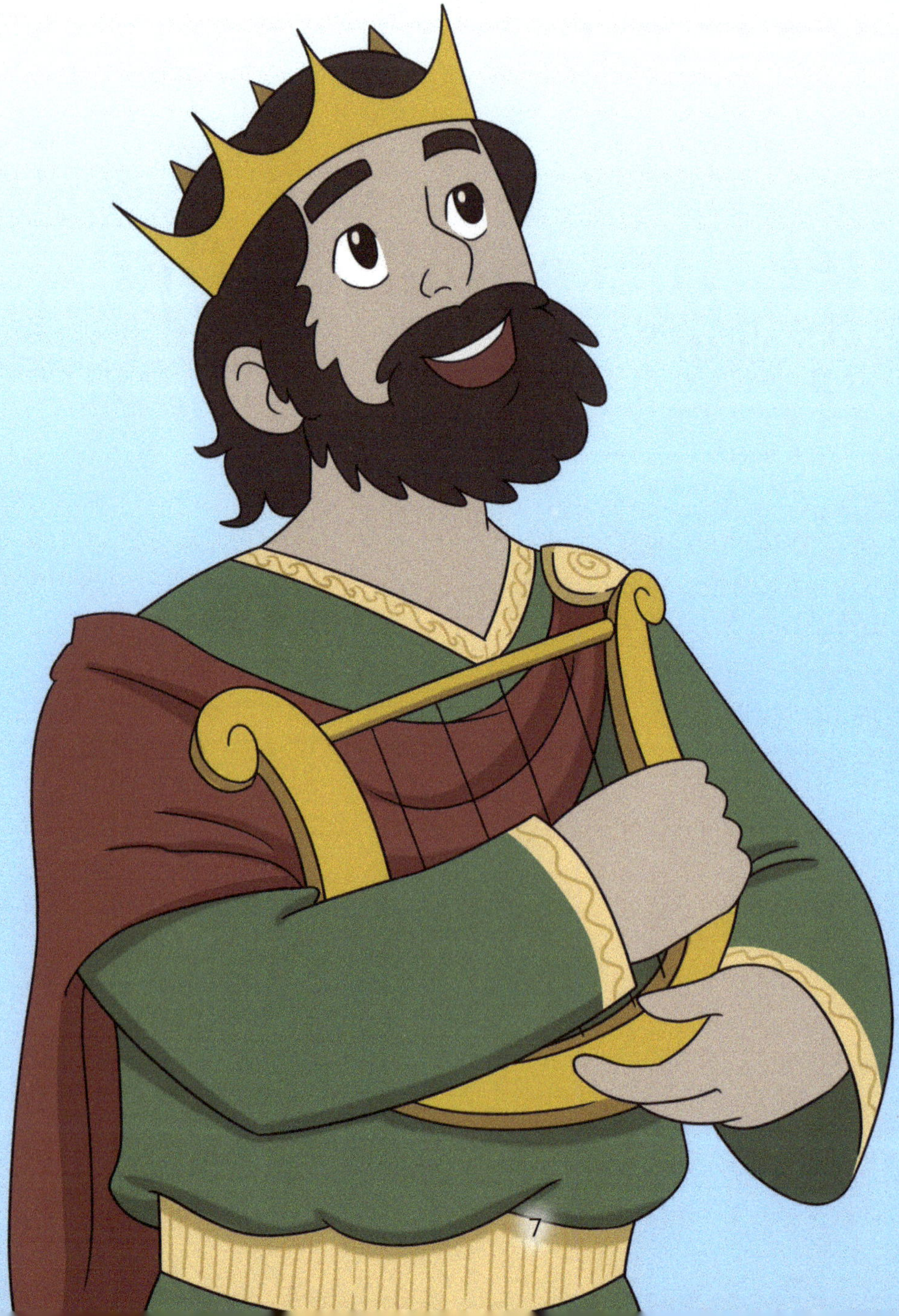

David as Family

(2 Samuel 8:1-15; Psalm 18; Luke 3:23-31; Acts 13:22; 1 Timothy 6:15)

The timeline in Luke shows that David is kin,
He was special to God and was honored by men.
King David could sing and did marvelous things,
But we all know that Jesus is King of all Kings.

Almighty God

Wonderful

Everlasting Father

Counselor

Prince of Peace

Everlasting Father

(Isaiah 9:6; Luke 1:35; John 10:30)

Isaiah speaks sure of the claims that he makes.
Our faith in his statements is all that it takes,
To see Christ's connection to God's deity.
He is one of the three in Blessed Trinity.

11

Fullness of the Godhead Bodily

(Proverbs 18:22; Colossians 2:9; I John 4:2)

As we look back in time at Jesus's life,
Joseph seeks out a modest, pure wife.
He loves his sweet Mary, but to his surprise,
God in the flesh would soon be her child.

13

Gabriel

(Luke 1:26–35)

He stated to Mary, "The Spirit's on you.
You truly are blessed and you're favored, too.
You'll be overshadowed by His power above,
To carry God's Son and be filled with His love."

15

Humble

(Luke 2:7; Philippians 2:5–8)

He was born in a Bethlehem stable so small,
with cows, sheep, and donkeys, at rest in a stall.
This marked the beginning of His humble life,
to reign as a King with no grumble or strife.

God with us

Immanuel

(Matthew 1:23; Isaiah 7:14)

His name was determined before He was born,
or swaddling clothes would ever be worn.
Immanuel, which God chose as His name,
and "God is with us" are one and the same.

19

Joseph

(Matthew 1:19–25; Luke 2:4, 5)

Joseph decided to follow the law.
From his firm commitment, he did not withdraw.
He followed the words that the angel said do,
To marry his Mary and love the child, too.

21

King Herod

(Matthew 2:1-8)

The king asked the kings about the young child.
The thought of King Jesus was driving him wild.
Although he was angry, he tried not to lose
his temper outright with the latest of news.

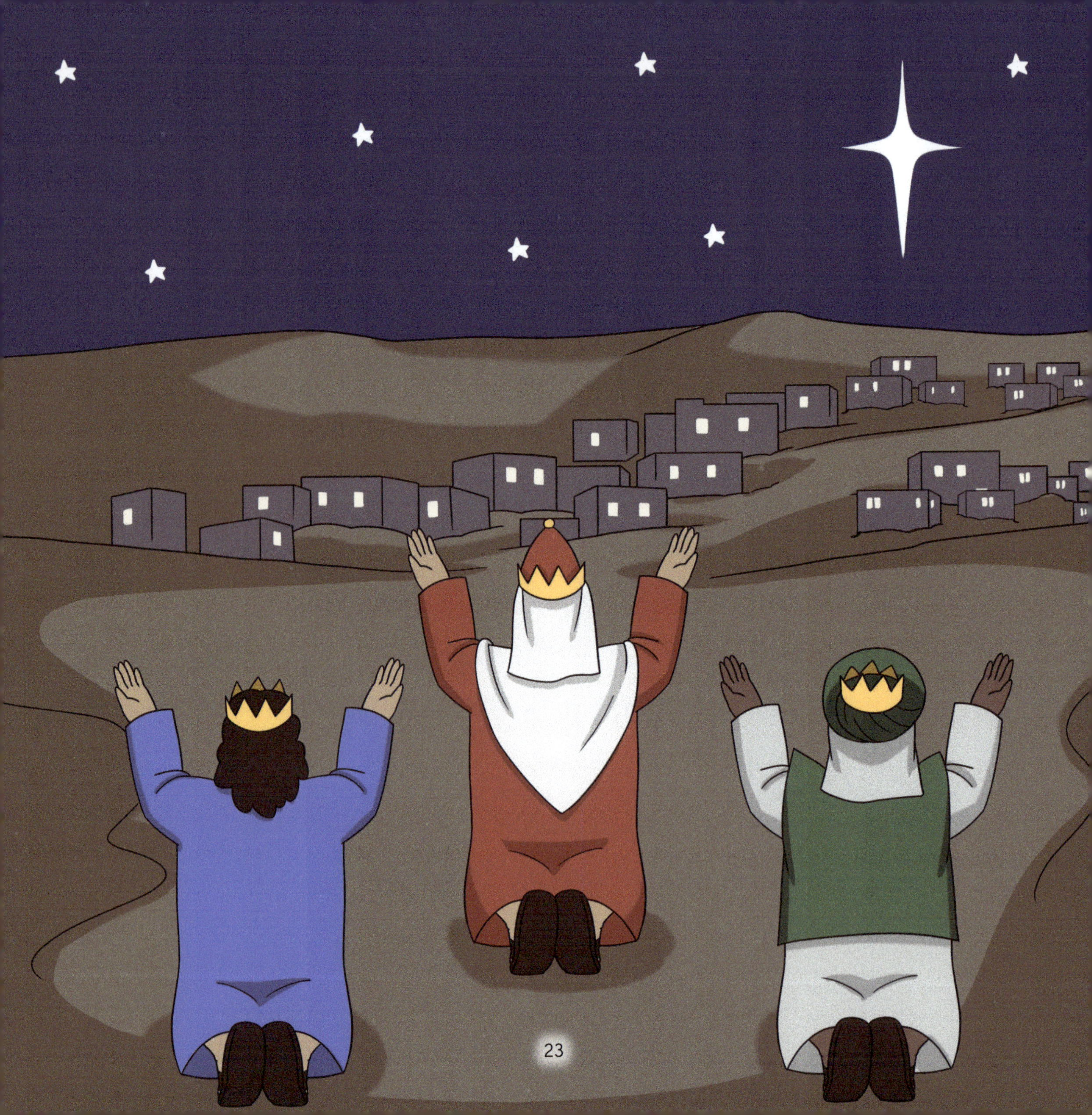

The Light of a Star

(Matthew 2:9–12)

They followed the star, no time did they waste.
The king and the shepherds all traveled with haste.
They dropped to their knees in worship and awe,
when the King of all Kings in the manger they saw.

25

Mary

(Luke 2:19)

She thought, as she laid her eyes upon Him,
He was a rare jewel, a real precious gem.
She pondered about the idea that she
was mother of Jesus by heaven's decree.

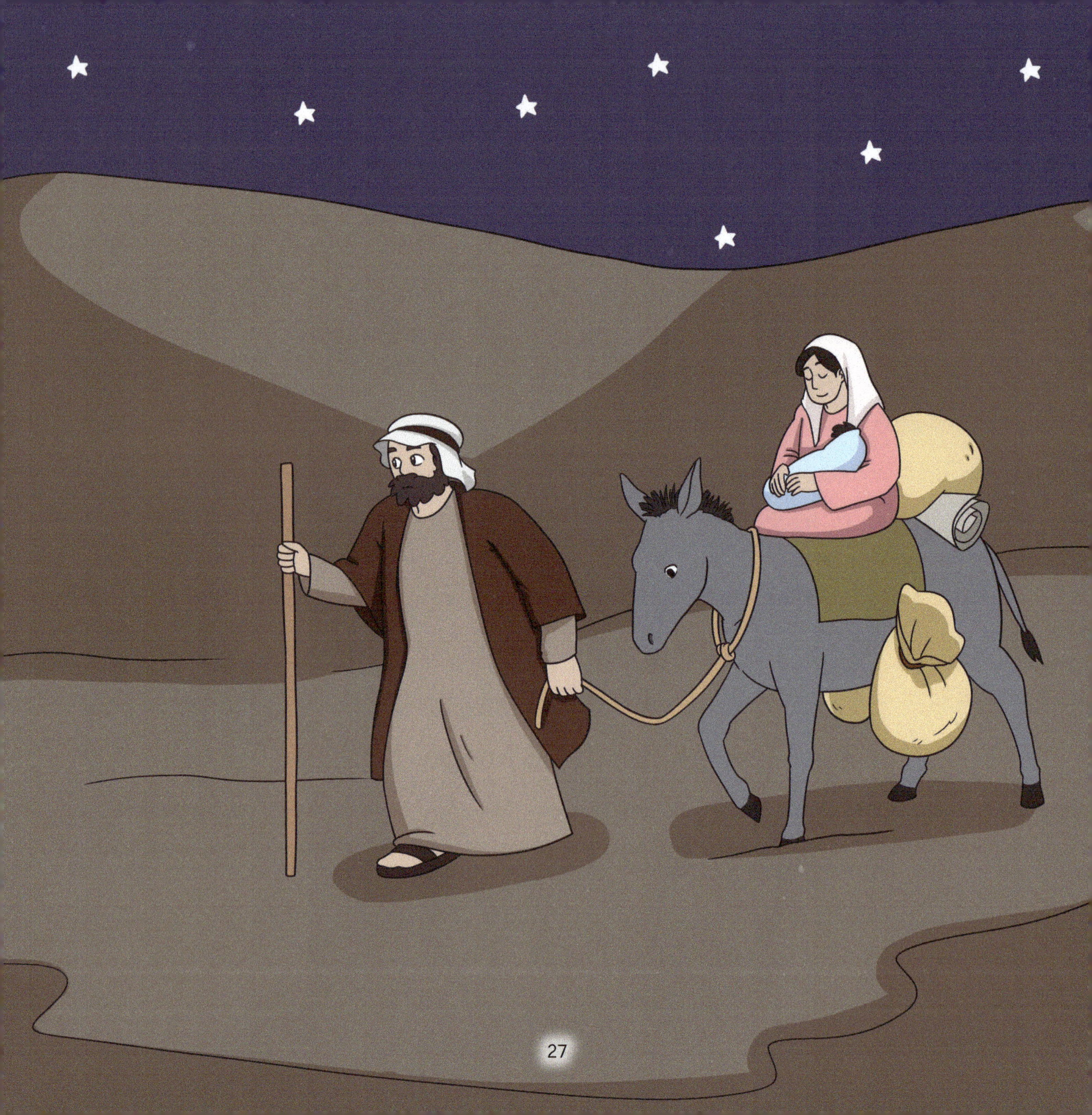

Night

(Matthew 2:12–14)

An angel warned Joseph King Herod was mad.
He killed very young boys and mothers were sad.
Slipping away to Egypt that night,
His parents and Jesus fled with all their might.

29

Out of Egypt

(Hosea 11: 1; Matthew 2:15, 21–23; Luke 1:32)

"Out of Egypt, I have called my Son,"
were words that were spoken by the Most High one.
Nazareth was His earthly abode.
From there, His story of love would be told.

31

Preacher

(Isaiah 61:1; Luke 4:18; Luke 5:15)

By the Spirit of God, the gospel He preached.
He spoke day and night, and thousands He reached.
The cast down, and brokenhearted, and poor,
heard His message of love and felt loved even more.

33

Question Asked by Jesus

(Matthew 16:13–16; Mark 8:27–29)

Simon was asked "Who do men say I am?"
He hoped they would see Him as Sacrificed Lamb.
"You are the Christ, the Son of God."
"Simon, you're blessed," Jesus said with a nod.

35

Rejected

(Matthew 26:56; Mark 14:71; Luke 4:24; John 7:5)

He was hailed and applauded in Jerusalem.
The crowds there gave glory and honor to Him.
But some of His family, and many a friend,
left His side as they fled when His life was to end.

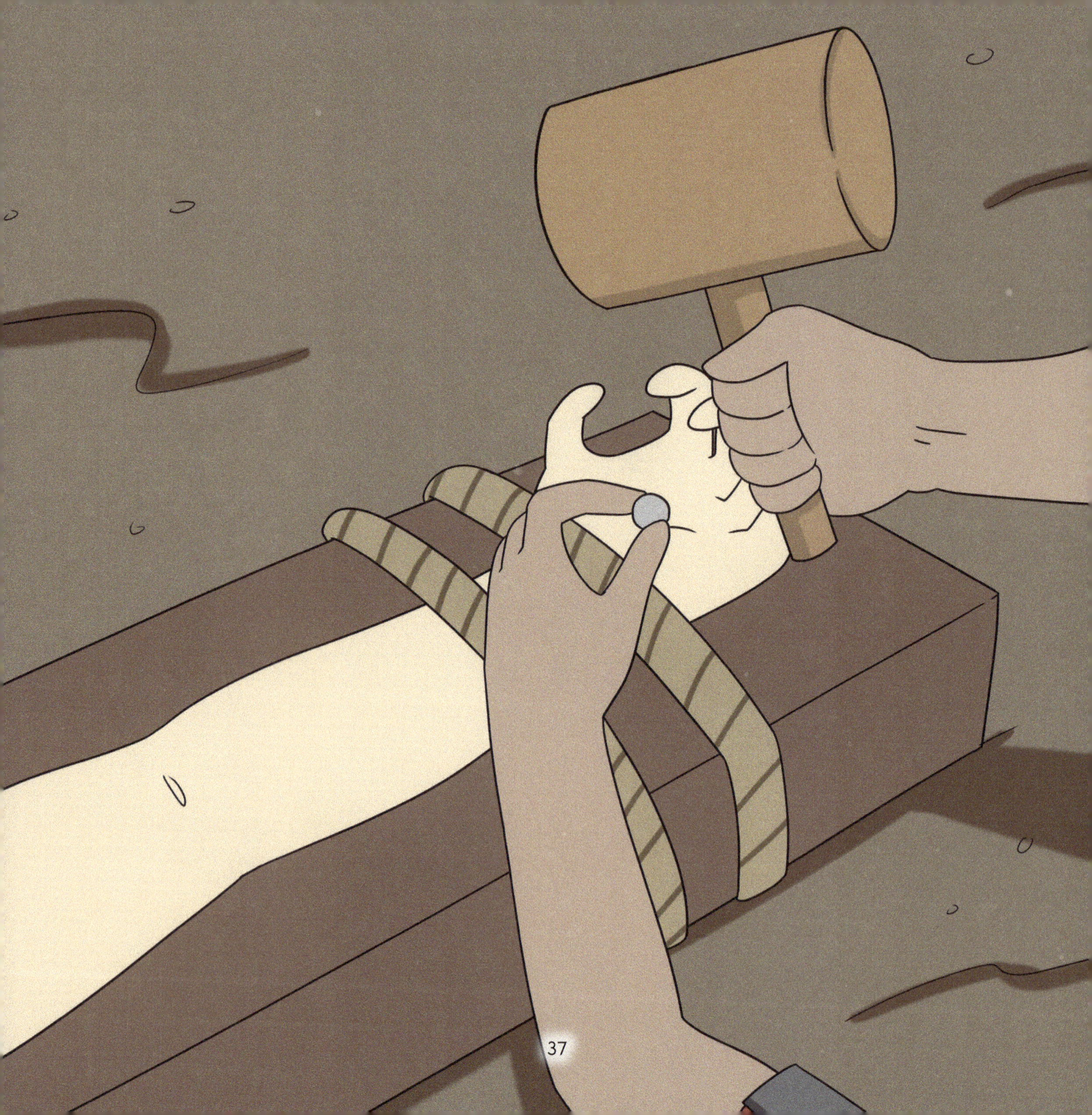

Savior

(Romans 5:8, 15; Ephesians 1:7; I John 3:5)

He suffered and died on the cross for our sins.
For our disobedience, He made amends.
His stripes, and His blood, and broken body,
was His way of showing He loved you and me.

39

Tomb

(Matthew 12:40; 27:57-28:8)

He had lain in the tomb for three days and three nights,
when suddenly there was a stream of bright lights.
An earthquake took place; the stone rolled away.
The angel saw Jesus rise up on that day.

41

Up

(Mark 16:19-20; Luke 24:50-53; Acts 2:1-6)

After promising to His disciples He'd send
a comfort, the Holy Spirit in wind,
He was taken to heaven; His place to reside.
He sits with His Father now on His right side.

43

Victory (over Death)

(I Corinthians 15; 54-56; Revelation 1:18)

He holds the key over death and of Hell.
He is not dead. He's alive and He's well.
If we take notice, and take a look,
we'll see that He wins at the end of the Book.

45

Worship

(Revelation 5:11–13)

Angels are worshiping around the throne,
they're always with Him; He's never alone.
They praise Him for He was the Lamb that was slain.
Forever and ever, He will always reign.

Our Father in Heaven
Hallowed be Thy name
Thy Kingdom come
Thy will be done
On Earth as it is in Heaven
Give us this day our daily bread
And forgive us our sins
As we forgive those who sin against us
Do not bring us into temptation
But deliver us from evil. Amen.

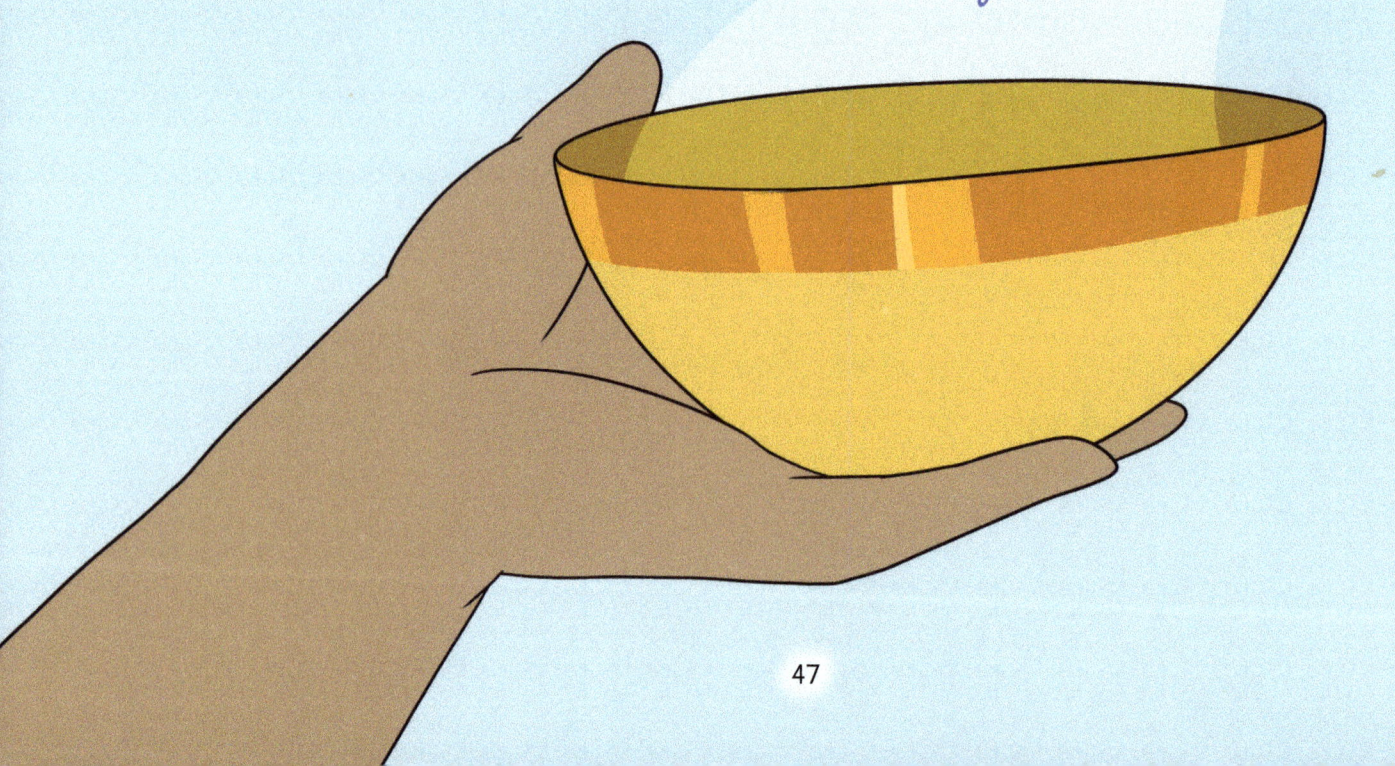

XXIV (24)

(Revelation 5:8-9)

They're twenty-four elders with harps and with bowls
that holds all our prayers poured out from our souls.
They sing "You are Worthy because You were slain;
Your blood has redeemed us from our sinful stains."

49

You

(Matthew 20:34; Mark 1:41; Luke 22:51; John 15:13)

He did all of this with YOU on His mind.
A much truer friend, you never will find.
He laid down His life, for He loves you so much.
Just reach out to Him; you'll be healed by His touch.

51

Zion

(Isaiah 24:23, 28:16; Psalm 132:13-14; Zechariah 2:10)

It is there we will live with Him evermore.
His dwelling place has many treasures in store.
In Zion, He is the Sure Cornerstone,
a place where we proudly will call it our own.

CPSIA information can be obtained
at www.ICGtesting.com
Printed in the USA
BVHW022021030321
601620BV00014B/129